THIS BOOK BELONGS TO

_____

ADVENTURES WITH A SPECIAL TRAVELER
Copyright © 2018 by Marla Murasko

ISBN 13: 978-0-9979317-8-5
ISBN 10: 0-9979317-8-7

Library of Congress PCN: 2018932241

All Rights Reserved. No parts of this book may be reproduced or utilized in any form or by any means, electronic or mechanical, including photocopying, scanning, recording, or by any information storage and retrieval system now known or hereafter invented, without permission, in writing from the publisher.

To contact Marla Murasko or to order a copy of this book, please visit **www.amitypublications.com.**

Design and Layout by
AMITY Publications
www.amitypublications.com

Printed in the United States of America

ADVENTURES WITH A SPECIAL TRAVELER

Written by Marla Murasko

Illustrated by Gabrielle Taylor Jensen

DEDICATED TO
MY DETERMINED AND CURIOUS SON...
JACOB

When Jacob was born, he was very fragile. Not only was he born with Down Syndrome, but he was also diagnosed with a congenital heart condition called "Tetralogy of Fallot." He had two major surgeries before the age of one. We knew we wanted him to live a full life, visiting family on the East Coast and enjoying family vacations all over the world. So, he took his first plane ride at nine months, just three months after open heart surgery. He hasn't stopped flying since.

Jacob loves to travel. He loves riding in the plane and visiting the captain when he can. He loves the whole process of taking a trip from packing his suitcase to going through security to unpacking in the hotel. He also loves the fun things like going out to dinners, swimming at the beach, playing golf, going to amusement parks and more!

We hope Jacob will inspire your family to travel and see the world.

A NOTE FROM THE AUTHOR...

When my husband and I met, we both loved to travel, eat out and enjoy life. We had dreams of traveling with our family as we both had enjoyed family vacations growing up in New Jersey.

We were very excited to learn I was finally pregnant. But within four months, we were told our son had a hole in his heart. We were also told statistics showed at my age, there was a 1/100 chance Jacob would have Down Syndrome as well. My husband and I agreed no matter the test results, we would continue our dream of having a family and vacations. We were determined to give our son every opportunity to enjoy life to its fullest.

I wrote this book about Jacob's love of traveling on an airplane in hopes of encouraging other families who have a child with a "special needs diagnosis" to continue to follow their dreams. It is possible. . .you just have to plan differently. The world is waiting for you. . . go out and enjoy.

All proceeds from this book will be donated to our non-profit organization "SPECIAL & DETERMINED (www.special-and-determined.com). We are dedicated to helping families of children with Down Syndrome by providing financial support for therapeutic services, early intervention and building a path to a more accepting and inclusive society where all individuals can contribute.

Marla Murasko

Jacob was very excited. His family was going on vacation.
You see, Jacob loves to travel. He loves to ride on buses and trains, but his favorite way to travel is riding on airplanes.

Jacob loves how big they are, how shiny they look, but mostly how fast they go.

Every day Jacob would ask Mommy,
"Is it time to go to the airport?"

"Not yet," answered Mommy. "Just a few more days," and they would count them on a calendar.

The day finally arrived. Jacob saw Mommy packing and knew it was time to get ready. He ran off to get his toothbrush, some books and his suitcase.

Jacob couldn't wait to get to the airport. As Mommy, Daddy, his sister Amanda and he walked toward security, Jacob saw a lot of people standing in line. Sometimes, this would scare him but not today. Jacob was so excited to be going on a trip.

Even though the man at the airport told him he could keep his shoes on, he liked to take them off like his big sister.
Jacob looked up at Amanda. "Shoes off?" he asked.
Amanda smiled and nodded her head.

Jacob eagerly sat on the floor and took off his shoes.
When he was done, Jacob jumped up and shouted,
"I'm ready!" and got in line with Amanda.

After his sister helped him put his shoes back on, Jacob grabbed his suitcase, reached for Mommy's hand and they started to walk through the airport.

They came to the tunnel with the moving stairs and the pretty lights on the ceiling. Jacob especially liked going down the moving stairs. As he got to the top of the stairs, he took his sister's hand. They counted, "1-2-3" and carefully stepped onto the stairs.

Once on the airplane, Jacob settled into his seat near the window. He was so excited. He knew the plane would be up in the clouds very soon.

The flight attendant came by and asked if Jacob and Amanda would like to see where the captain sits. Jacob jumped up with a big smile on his face and shouted, "YES!"

Amanda and Jacob headed toward the man standing in the front of the plane.
"Hi. I'm Captain Pete," he said. "I thought you might like to see where I sit on the airplane."

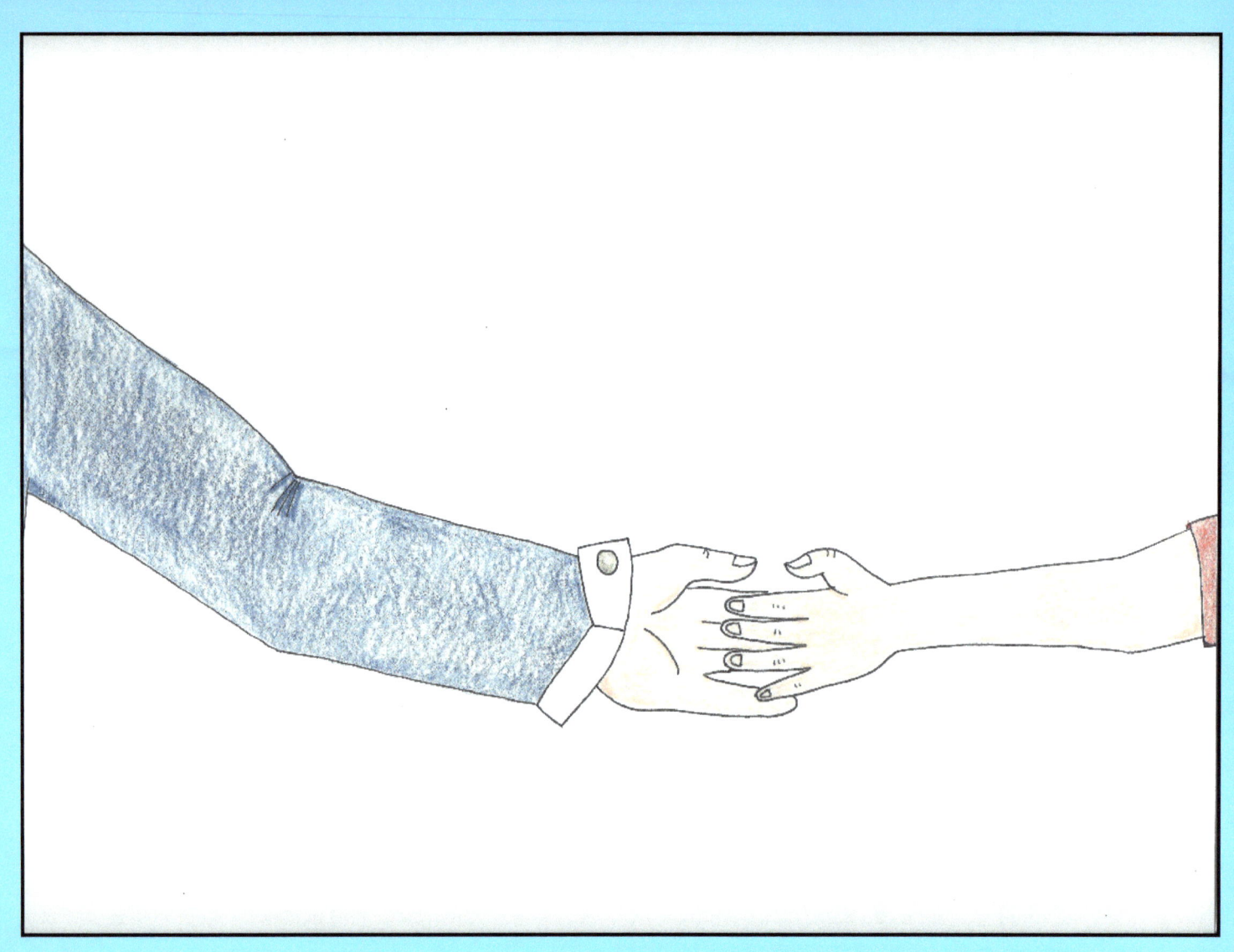

Jacob was so excited to meet the captain.
He put out his hand and said, "Hi, I'm Jacob."

The captain showed them the cockpit. He explained some of the buttons, lights and handles. Then he asked if Jacob would like to sit in the pilot's seat. Jacob nodded "yes."

Amanda picked up her brother and sat him in the captain's seat. Jacob grabbed the handles of the steering wheel as he pretended he was flying the plane. Jacob looked at the captain and said, "Fast." The captain laughed and said, "Yes, this plane goes fast."

"It's time to go back to your seats," the flight attendant told Amanda and Jacob. The captain shook their hands and gave Jacob a pair of plastic wings. "This is for my Junior Pilot," he said. Jacob grinned from ear to ear.

Jacob showed everyone his wings as he walked back to his seat. Daddy said they were really cool. He was so proud of Jacob.

Jacob buckled his seatbelt. As the plane taxied down the runway, Daddy told Jacob it was time for the plane to take off. Jacob loved going up in the sky and started counting, "5, 4, 3, 2, 1. . . up!"

Once the plane was in the clouds, Jacob settled down to watch movies on his tablet. It wasn't long before a voice came over the loud speaker.

"We will be landing soon. I wanted to say a special thank you to my Junior Pilot Jacob for helping me fly the plane," announced the captain. Jacob couldn't stop smiling. Everyone was clapping as he shouted, "That's me!"

Thanks to so many people who help him feel special and make him feel safe, Jacob loves to travel, especially on an airplane.

MEET
JACOB MURASKO

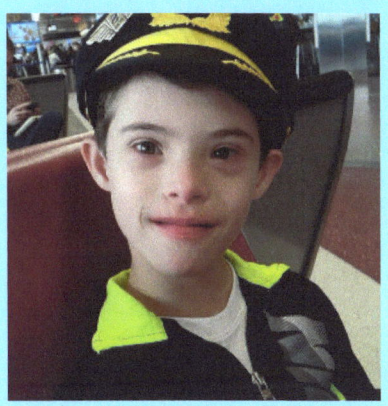

Hi. My name is Jacob Murasko. I am 11 years old. I was born in Illinois. I lived in Indiana and now live in Massachusetts. I am in the 5th grade. I like spending time with my family and friends. I love playing basketball. I love watching Notre Dame football, basketball and, of course, the marching band. I love music, playing golf with my dad, singing with my mom, being goofy with my sister, and playing with my dog Bella! And oh yeah...I love traveling!!!

I love meeting new people and, according to my parents, I seem to touch the lives of all those I meet. I like when my Mom comes to my school to talk to my friends about me. You see, I have "Down Syndrome". I know I need some extra help with my school work and things may be a little harder for me but I always keep trying.

I have dreams of going to college and having a job. Maybe someday I will be able to work at Notre Dame or on a golf course. But mostly I hope to keep traveling. I get to see and do so many new things. If I could tell you one thing, I would say, "Get a passport. I love having mine. Oh yeah, and don't forget to start collecting your wings like I do."

Jacob's collection of "wings" along with his Passport.

DOWN SYNDROME

In 1866 British physician, John Langdon Down, for whom the syndrome is now named, first described Down syndrome, as "Mongolism." The term Down Syndrome didn't become the accepted term until the early 1970s.

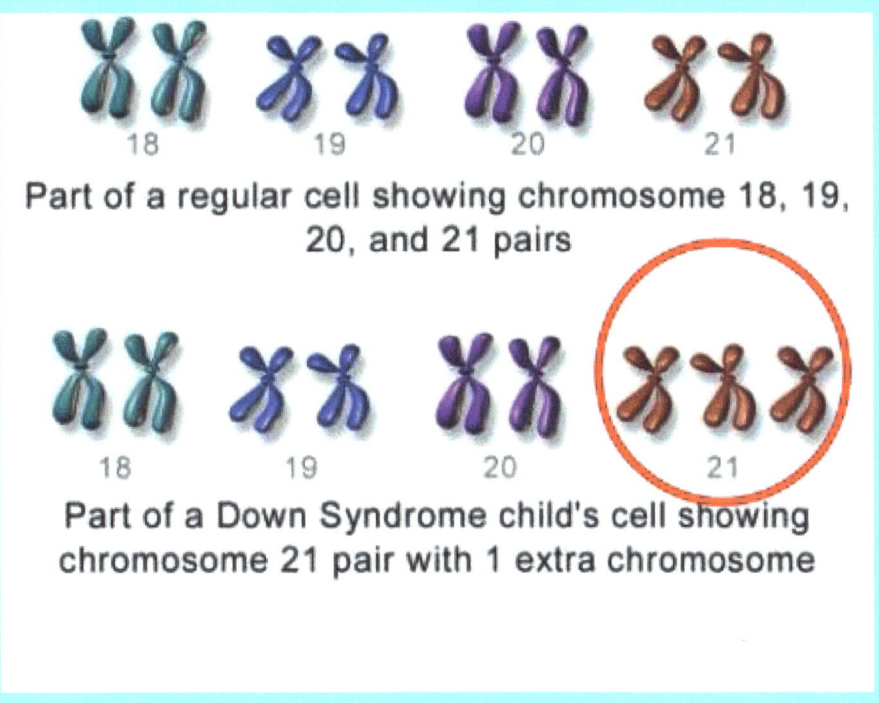

ABOUT DOWN SYNDROME

1. Down Syndrome is a common condition caused by having "extra" copies of genes on the 21st chromosome (American Academy of Pediatrics) *(1)*

2. Neuro-typical individuals have 46 chromosomes an individual diagnosed with Down Syndrome has 47.

3. According to the Centers for Disease Control and Prevention, approximately one in every 700 babies in the United States is born with Down Syndrome, making Down Syndrome the most common chromosomal condition. About 6,000 babies with Down Syndrome are born in the United States each year. *(2)*

4. Many people with Down Syndrome have the common facial features and no other major birth defects. However, some people with Down Syndrome might have one or more major birth defects or other medical problems. Some of the more common health problems among children with Down Syndrome are listed below. *(3)*

   - Hearing loss (up to 75% of people with Down Syndrome may be affected)
   - Obstructive sleep apnea, which is a condition where the person's breathing temporarily stops while asleep (between 50-75%)
   - Ear infections (between 50 -70%)
   - Eye diseases (up to 60%), like cataracts and eye issues requiring glasses
   - Heart defects present at birth (50%)

5. A few of the common physical traits of Down Syndrome are low muscle tone, small stature, an upward slant to the eyes, and a single deep crease across the center of the palm. Every person with Down Syndrome is a unique individual and may possess these characteristics to different degrees or not at all.

6. People with Down Syndrome attend school, work, participate in decisions that affect them, and contribute to society in many wonderful ways.

7. All people with Down Syndrome experience intellectual disabilities and some physical challenges, but the effect is usually mild to moderate and is not indicative of the many strengths and talents that each individual possesses.

8. Quality educational programs, a stimulating home environment, good health care, and positive support from family, friends and the community enable people with Down Syndrome to develop their full potential and lead fulfilling lives.

References

1. Health Care Information for Families of Children with Down Syndrome: http://www.ndsccenter.org/wp-content/uploads/AAP-Health-Care-Information-for-Families-of-Children-with-Down-Syndrome.pdf

2. Parker SE, Mai CT, Canfield MA, et al. Updated national birth prevalence estimates for selected birth defects in the United States, 2004-2006. Birth Defects Res A Clin Mol Teratol. 2010, 88:1008-16.

3. Bull MJ, the Committee on Genetics. Health supervision for children with Down syndrome. Pediatrics. 2011, 128:393-406.

HELPFUL RESOURCES

National Down Syndrome Society (NDSS)
www.ndss.org

is the leading human rights organization for all individuals
with Down Syndrome

National Down Syndrome Congress (NDSC)
www.ndccenter.org

provides information, advocacy and support concerning
all aspects of life for individuals with Down syndrome.

National Association for Down Syndrome (NADS)
www.nads.org
supports all persons with Down Syndrome in achieving their full potential.

Global Down Syndrome Foundation
www.globaldownsyndrome.org
works to educate governments, educational organizations and society
in order to affect legislative and social changes so that every person
with Down Syndrome has an equitable chance at a satisfying life.

SPECIAL NEEDS TRAVEL INFORMATION

Here is a list of resources to help you when arranging travel for your special needs child:

1) Visit TSA Cares Helpline: (855) 787-2227 or visit their website at https://www.tsa.gov/travel/passenger-support for any questions about carrying medicine in carry-ons, going through the screening process. Call 72 hours prior to traveling with questions about screening policies, procedures and what to expect at the security checkpoint.

2) Passenger Support Specialists have advanced training supporting an individual with a disability or a medical condition with "on the spot" service depending on availability at the airport.

3) Check out the Special Needs Assistance information for these airlines:

American Airlines   Delta   JetBlue   Southwest   United Airlines

Wings For Autism - http://www.thearc.org/wingsforautism

Visit our website http://adventureswithaspecialtraveler.com
for more information on special needs travel.

THE END of the story...
but not the end of traveling for Jacob.

www.ingramcontent.com/pod-product-compliance
Lightning Source LLC
Chambersburg PA
CBHW041538040426

42446CB00002B/136